A Visit to
ISRAEL

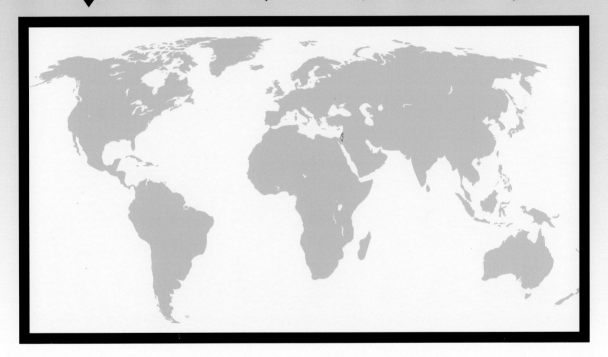

Peter & Connie Roop

Heinemann Library
Chicago, Illinois

Designed by AMR
Illustrations by Art Construction
Printed in Hong Kong / China

02 01
10 9 8 7 6 5 4 3

Library of Congress Cataloging-in-Publication Data

Roop, Peter.
    Israel / Peter Roop, Connie Roop.
       p.   cm.
    Summary: Introduces the land, landmarks, homes, food, clothes,
work, transportation, language, and culture of Israel.
    ISBN 1-57572-711-0 (library binding)
    1. Israel--Description and travel--Juvenile literature.
[1. Israel.] I. Roop, Connie. II. Title.
DS107.5.R66   1998
956.94--dc21   98-12449
                                                                                            CIP
                                                                                            AC

Acknowledgments
The Publishers would like to thank the following for permission to reproduce photographs:
J. Allan Cash: pp. 7, 10, 11, 12, 16, 17, 20; Hutchison Library: p. 13, R. Francis p. 25, M. Friend p. 14,
J. Henderson p. 18; Images Color Library: pp. 8, 9; Israel Tourist Office: p. 29; Magnum: Abbas pp.21, 24,
F. Mayer p. 22, D. Stock p. 19; Panos Pictures: H. Davies pp. 15, 23, G. Mansfield p. 6; Performing Arts
Library: C. Barda p. 28; Trip: H. Rogers p. 27, S. Shapiro p. 26, A. Tovy p. 5

Cover photograph reproduced with permission of Carlos Reyes-Manzo Andes Press Agency

Every effort has been made to contact copyright holders of any material reproduced in this
book. Any omissions will be rectified in subsequent printings if notice is given to the Publisher.

Any words appearing in bold, **like this,** are explained in the Glossary.

Contents

Israel

MEDITERRANEAN SEA

North

Jerusalem

Dead Sea

ISRAEL

Negev Desert

Red Sea

Key
- Land above 3,300 ft/1000 m
- Land above 0 ft/m/sea level
- Land below 0 ft/m/sea level
- ● Capital

Israel is one of the smallest countries in the world. The modern country of Israel was formed in 1948.

Although **Arab** people lived there, it was given to the **Jewish** people. They came from all around the world to live there. Israelis eat, sleep, play, and go to school like you. Israeli life is also **unique**.

Land

Israel has mountains, **valleys,** and **deserts.** Half of the country is in the Negev Desert.

Israel has hot, dry summers. Winters are cool and wet. This good weather helps the farmers to grow large **crops** of fruits and vegetables.

Landmarks

The Dead Sea is so salty that fish and plants can't live in it. All the salt in the water stops people from sinking. They just float on top!

Jerusalem is Israel's **capital** and its largest and oldest city. People have lived there for 5,000 years. It is a holy city for **Jews, Christians,** and **Muslims.**

Homes

In the cities, most people live in small apartments or houses. There is not much space for them to have back yards.

In the country, people live on their own farms or *kibbutzim*. *Kibbutzim* are where many families live and work together as one large family.

Food

Much of the food in Israel is kosher.
Kosher means that food is prepared and
served following special **Jewish** rules.
Lunch is the main meal of the day.

Fruit and vegetables are eaten with every meal. *Felafel* (fell-LAH-fell) is a favorite dish. It is a fried food made from chickpeas.

Clothes

Most Israelis wear clothes like yours.
In the hot weather, they wear cooler,
cotton clothes.

Some **Jews** wear black hats and clothes as part of their **religion**. **Arabs** often wear robes and **headdresses**.

Work

Farmers have learned how to grow **crops** in the **desert**. The farmers are very careful not to waste water. They grow cotton, wheat, fruit, vegetables, and olives.

Most of Israel's factories are in the cities.
The factory workers make machines,
weapons, radios, televisions, computers,
and cloth.

Transportation

Israel is small. It does not take long to travel from one end to the other by bus or car. There are airplanes and trains, too.

Bedouins in the Negev **Desert** use
donkeys to carry their loads. Bedouins
move their tents from place to place
to find water for their animals.

Language

Four out of five people in Israel are Jewish. **Jews** speak and write Hebrew, the **ancient** Jewish language. Signs are written in Hebrew, Arabic, and English.

Most of the non-Jews in Israel are **Arabs.**
They speak and write Arabic. This language
has 28 letters. Like Hebrew, it is read from
right to left.

School

Jewish children go to school every day, except Saturday. Saturday is their day to rest, play, and pray. At school children study Hebrew, Arabic, math, science, history, and English.

Arab children have their own schools.
Their day off is Sunday. They study math,
science, history, Arabic, and English.

Free Time

Soccer is the most popular sport in Israel. Many people enjoy basketball and tennis, too.

Many Israelis take long walks in the countryside or help on farms and *kibbutzim*. At the Red Sea they enjoy water sports, such as **snorkeling,** swimming, and windsurfing.

Celebrations

Rosh Hashanah is the **Jewish** New Year. It is celebrated in September for two days. Children and their families enjoy special foods like apples and honey.

Hanukkah is the Jewish festival of lights. It takes place in winter for eight nights. People light special candles. There is one candle for every night of the festival.

The Arts

Israelis enjoy going to a play or a concert. Many famous musicians, such as Zubin Mehta, have come from Israel.

Singing and dancing are also very popular.
Many Israelis dance the **hora** in parks on
Saturday evenings. Movies are a favorite
indoor entertainment.

Fact File

Name The full name of Israel is the State of Israel.

Capital The **capital** city of Israel is Jerusalem.

Languages Most Israelis speak Hebrew, Arabic, or English.

Population There are more than 5 million people living in Israel.

Money Instead of the dollar, the Israelis have the *shekel*.

Religions Most Israelis believe in Judaism or **Islam**.

Products Israel produces lots of machines, diamonds, chemicals, cloth, fruit, and vegetables.

Words You Can Learn

ehhad (eh-KHAD)	one
shtayim	two
shalosh (sha-LOSH)	three
shalom (sha-LOM)	hello, goodbye
todah (to-DAH)	thank you
bevkasha (be-va-ka-SHA)	please
ken	yes
loh	no

Glossary

ancient	from a long time ago
Arab	the people living in north Africa or western parts of Asia (called the Middle East)—many of them are Muslims
Bedouin	a group of people that lives in tents in the desert
capital	the city where the government is based
Christians	the people who believe in Jesus Christ
crops	the plants that farmers grow
deserts	large areas of land that have little or no rain and very few plants or animals
headdresses	pieces of cloth tied around the head
hora	a well-known Jewish dance that can be danced in a circle
Islam	the religion of the Arabs
Jews	the people who believe in the Judaic religion
Muslims	the people who believe in the Islamic religion
religion	what people believe in
snorkeling	swimming under water with breathing equipment
temple	a building used as a place of worship
unique	different in a special way
valleys	the low areas between hill tops or mountains

Index

More Books to Read

Allard, Denise. *Israel*. Chatham, NJ: Raintree Steck-Vaughn. 1997.

Baily, Donna. *Israel*. Chatham, NJ: Raintree Steck-Vaughn. 1990.

Bickman, Connie. *Children of Israel*. Minneapolis, MN: Abdo & Daughters Publishing. 1994.

King, David C. *Israel*. Vero Beach, FL: Rourke Book Company, Inc. 1995. An older reader can help you with this book.